SURPLUS

FEARLESS GENEROSITY
IN 2 CORINTHIANS 8-9

BRYAN ELLIFF

Surplus: Fearless Generosity in 2 Corinthians 8-9
Bryan Elliff

Copyright © 2019 by Bryan Elliff

This first edition published by Christian Communicators Worldwide.

CHRISTIAN COMMUNICATORS WORLDWIDE
P. O. Box 12045
Parkville, MO 64152

www.ccwtoday.org

Cover and interior design by Tony Barmann.
All rights reserved.

Purchase additional copies of this book at Amazon.com.
For information about this and other publications
write info@ccwtoday.org.

Scripture taken from the NEW AMERICAN STANDARD BIBLE®,
Copyright © 1960, 1962, 1963, 1968, 1971, 1972, 1973, 1975, 1977,
1995 by the Lockman Foundation. Used by permission.
www.lockman.org

ISBN 978-0-9745253-6-5

CONTENTS

remaining chapters will include reading the smaller Scripture portion before the chapter, and the chapter itself. You may even wish to sometimes ask the participants to read the two chapters in 2 Corinthians repeatedly at home to enhance the study. Application questions follow each chapter. Please add your own questions as time allows.

Will you help us get this truth out?

We hope that you will see the value in this serious approach to Bible study written in an accessible way. If you are able, please write a brief review on Amazon, or recommend that others you know study the book. We are offering deep discounts for multiple copies on our site also (www.ccwtoday.org). Perhaps some of you would be able to pass your copy of this book around or give away multiple copies so that this joy of giving may be caught by others.

We're so glad you are reading *Surplus*. We're excited about this book and the books that will follow over the next years in the Bristol Series. The Bristol Series is for thinking Christians who really desire to study single passages in a deeper way, complete with background information and careful attention to the context and details of the passage.

Studying this book with others? Here's what we recommend:

For weekly group study, we suggest *reading the chapters aloud together* rather than reading them at home individually between meetings. You may even wish to collect the books and redistribute them each time you meet until the class is completed. Then you can give them to the participants to hopefully share with others. For an even better Bible experience, you may wish to read aloud the full text in the back of the book each week before reading the smaller Scripture portion and the chapter for that session. This will orient the group if any were missing, and will deepen understanding and discussion.

The first lesson should include reading the Introduction, the full Bible text at the end of the book, and Chapter One. That's slightly more reading than

An Important Introduction

I remember when I first took seriously the Bible's teaching on money and possessions. I was a college student at home for the summer and Jesus' Sermon on the Mount was a topic of vigorous discussion among my friends. As I read and talked about those fascinating and memorable words of Christ, I realized just how uncomfortably countercultural they were. We noticed that we had a strange tendency to nuance his meaning into oblivion; Jesus surely did not mean what it sounded like he meant. On the one side, we valiantly tried to rescue him from being too severe or demanding. On the other side, his words propelled us toward a new kind of obedience. I bounced between common sense and uncommon words, wondering just how it could be possible to follow his principles as a twenty-first century American.

This kind of struggle is inevitable when we pay serious attention to Jesus and the other Bible authors as they write about money and possessions. That is because this subject, like few others, meets us in the practice of daily life.

It shoulders its way in and takes a seat at our kitchen table. Face to face with such personal instruction, we wake up to the Bible's countercultural call. That call makes us squirm at times, but it holds within it tremendous potential for growth and increased joy. The wrestling makes us stronger, pushing us to more courageous faith and sacrificial love.

In this book, we will revisit one of the New Testament's compelling stories, alluded to in three of its books and featured prominently in a fourth. The Apostle Paul, responding to a crisis of poverty among the believers in Jerusalem, undertook the arduous project of raising a collection for them among the young churches in the Roman provinces of modern-day Turkey and Greece. As we engage this story, we will focus our attention on 2 Corinthians, a letter Paul wrote around the mid-50s A.D. to the Christians in Corinth. In it he devotes two chapters to the subject of the collection (chapters 8-9). Working through these chapters, we will learn why he was so passionate about this undertaking and discover timeless principles about lack and liberality and how God's grace operates at the intersection of the two.

Paul's vision of generosity is surprising. He opens our eyes wide to an expansive landscape of liberality which does not begin or end with us. We find ourselves standing in the middle of something far larger—God's own generous program. This fresh perspective will motivate us.

A Christian leader once said, "Most of us only give enough to be miserable." That may be true. Most of us have yet to experience the overflowing joy that results from radical generosity. There is something more for us here, if we will listen with the intent to follow.

The full text of 2 Corinthians 8-9 is included in the back of this book. Please read it now. Also, be careful to read the smaller portion of 2 Corinthians 8-9 that precedes each chapter. Unlike many books, these passages are not add-ons, but essential to understanding.

Finally, pray as you read and determine to follow Christ's leadership in all things. That is how change comes.

Bryan Elliff
Los Angeles, CA

CCW's Bristol Series is for thinking Christians. We aim to provide readable, exegetically careful, and background-rich treatments of single texts of Scripture designed to speak strongly to critical issues in the life of believers. They are accompanied by discussion questions for study groups and mentoring.

Christian Communicators Worldwide, ccwtoday.org

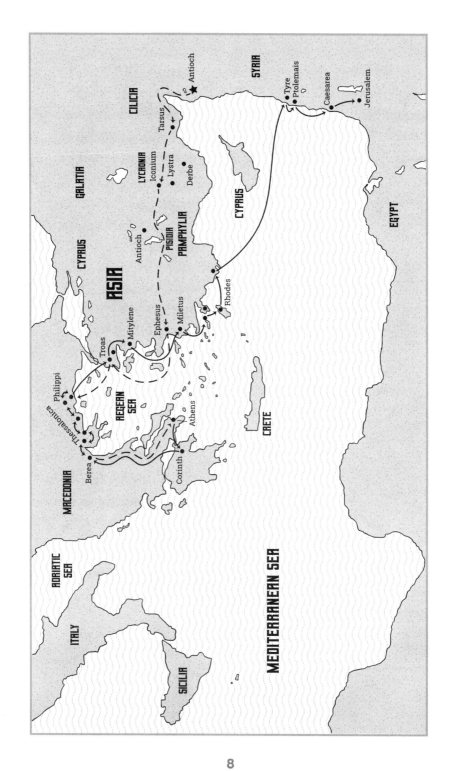

8

CHAPTER ONE

The Collection for the Saints in Jerusalem: The Story Begins

The disrupting yet joy-producing principles about grace and surplus just ahead are found in real-life experiences of lack and generosity. Join me now as I retell a story two millennia old.

When Paul wrote 2 Corinthians, around the year A.D. 56, the people in the churches of Judea were in financial crisis. No one is sure of the cause of their poverty, but we may speculate that it was tied to a famine which struck the area several years earlier. Before that event, in one of his classic dramatic moments, a prophet named Agabus stood up and predicted the famine in front of the believers in Antioch of Syria.

> Now at this time some prophets came down from Jerusalem to Antioch. One of them named Agabus stood up and began to indicate by the Spirit that there would

certainly be a great famine all over the world. And this took place in the reign of Claudius. And in the proportion that any of the disciples had means, each of them determined to send a contribution for the relief of the brethren living in Judea. And this they did, sending it in charge of Barnabas and Saul to the elders. (Acts 11:27-30)

If the account of the first-century Jewish historian Josephus is reliable, the famine severely affected the area of Jerusalem and Judea (the region around Jerusalem). In his words, "there was a famine in the land that overtook them [i.e. the people of Jerusalem], and many people died of starvation."[1] In response, Paul and Barnabas carried an initial contribution from the believers in Antioch to Jerusalem in order to help take the edge off of the crisis, as we just read.

The famine happened around A.D. 46, approximately 10 years before Paul composed 2 Corinthians 8-9 in A.D. 56. Given this time gap, we cannot be absolutely certain that the famine's lingering effects were the cause of the poverty crisis in Judea, but we know that these were worrisome days for them, regardless.

This is why, when Paul set out from Antioch on his third missionary journey around A.D. 52, he carried with him something more than his usual burden for the growing churches of Europe and Asia Minor (modern-day Turkey). This time he went with the added intention of taking up a collection for the struggling churches of Judea, the Jewish

---

[1] Josephus, *The Antiquities of the Jews*, 20:2:5.

seedbed of the Christian movement. He hoped that the largely Gentile congregations in the Roman provinces far from Jerusalem would contribute generously, both meeting a severe need as well as strengthening a sometimes-tenuous unity with their Jewish-born Christian brothers on the other end of the Roman world.

The Backstory Continues

We see the first mention of this collection in 1 Corinthians, which Paul likely wrote in Ephesus on the coast of Asia (western Turkey today), after walking through the region of Galatia (central Turkey). Paul would later travel on to Macedonia (northern Greece) with a plan to eventually arrive at the cosmopolitan city of Corinth in the south of the country, which at that time was even larger and more prominent than Athens, 52 miles away (see map on page 8).

In that first letter to the Corinthians, Paul gave specific instructions about how the money should be collected. He urged them, as he had evidently also urged the Galatians, to save up for it weekly, so that they would have an abundant gift to send on to Jerusalem whenever he arrived.

> Now concerning the collection for the saints, as I directed the churches of Galatia, so do you also. On the first day of every week each one of you is to put aside and save, as he may prosper, so that no collections be made when I come. When I arrive, whomever you may approve, I will send them with letters to carry your gift to Jerusalem; and if it is fitting for me to go also, they will go with me. But I will come to you after I go through

Macedonia, for I am going through Macedonia; and perhaps I will stay with you, or even spend the winter, so that you may send me on my way wherever I may go. (1 Corinthians 16:1-6)

Paul apparently felt that a collection taken up incrementally, over time, would be more bountiful and less pressured than one collected all at once when he got to the city.

Paul expected to come to Corinth soon, after stopping in Macedonia. At that time, the whole gift would be collected and Paul would either send it on to Jerusalem with delegates chosen by the Corinthians or else travel with them himself (see map on page 8).

This, then, is the context of 2 Corinthians 8-9 and Paul's ambitious experiment. What lies ahead will challenge our lives and recalibrate our thinking about surplus, lack, and liberality. We will pick up the story now that Paul is in Macedonia, where the churches have been unexpectedly generous. He is writing once again to Corinth to make sure that everything is arranged before his arrival.

Did the Project Succeed?

Before we proceed, we should look beyond 2 Corinthians 8-9 and ask: was Paul's project ultimately successful? It appears that it was. We can at least be sure that both the Macedonians and the Corinthians gave to the collection in the end, just as Paul had hoped. We know this because of what Paul says in Romans, which he writes once he is finally in Corinth and about to carry the collection on to Jerusalem (see map on page 8).

. . . but now, I am going to Jerusalem serving the saints. For Macedonia and Achaia have been pleased to make a contribution for the poor among the saints in Jerusalem. Yes, they were pleased to do so, and they are indebted to them. For if the Gentiles have shared in their spiritual things, they are indebted to minister to them also in material things. (Romans 15:25-27)

"Macedonia and Achaia" are the regions we are concerned with here. Macedonia (in northern Greece) is where Paul was when he wrote 2 Corinthians 8-9, and Achaia (in southern Greece) is the region where Corinth was. Looking back, now that he has visited both of those places and is about to travel on to Jerusalem, Paul says that they were in fact "pleased to make a contribution."

Yet, despite this initial success, Paul betrays in the following verses of Romans that he is feeling somewhat apprehensive about how the collection be received when it arrives in Jerusalem. Maybe he was worried that a gift from the "Gentiles" might not go over well with the Jewish mother church. Observe how he asks the Romans to pray that his "service for Jerusalem" (the collection) may prove "acceptable to the saints" (the Jewish believers in Jerusalem).

Now I urge you, brethren, by our Lord Jesus Christ and by the love of the Spirit, to strive together with me in your prayers to God for me, that I may be rescued from those who are disobedient in Judea, and that my service for Jerusalem may prove acceptable to the saints . . . (Romans 15:30-31)

We may never quite know how things went when Paul finally arrived in Jerusalem, gift in hand, except for one hint in Acts 21:17: "After we arrived in Jerusalem, the brethren received us gladly."

But we are getting ahead of ourselves. Paul has not yet arrived in Corinth and is writing 2 Corinthians 8-9 to discuss the issue of the collection with the believers there. Open your mind now to this rich passage and the remarkable story surrounding it.

Timeline of Events[2]

Famine strikes Judea	C. A.D. 46
Paul begins third missionary journey	Spring A.D. 52
Paul spends three years in Ephesus (writes 1 Corinthians during this time)	Summer A.D. 52 - Summer A.D. 55
Paul ministers in Macedonia (writes 2 Corinthians during this time)	Fall A.D. 55 - Summer A.D. 56
Paul ministers in Corinth (writes Romans during this time)	Fall A.D. 56 - Spring A.D. 57
Paul returns to Jerusalem with the collection	Spring A.D. 57

---

[2] All dates are approximate. In the interest of consistency, they follow the dates given in Eckhard J. Schnabel, *Paul the Missionary: Realities, Strategies and Methods* (Downers Grove, IL: InterVarsity Press, 2008).

Questions for Discussion

Before discussing these questions, it is best to have read the Introduction, the text of 2 Corinthians 8-9 (found in the back), and Chapter One of this book.

1. What are some of the most immediately impressive verses of 2 Corinthians 8-9? Read these verses aloud and briefly share why you noticed them.
2. What parts of 2 Corinthians 8-9 appear at first to be the most difficult to understand and apply?
3. What are some of the things you anticipate you might learn from a study of this text?
4. What is confusing about the background story recounted in Chapter One that could be clarified? Discuss clarifications.

Now, brethren, we wish to make known to you the grace of God which has been given in the churches of Macedonia, that in a great ordeal of affliction their abundance of joy and their deep poverty overflowed in the wealth of their liberality. For I testify that according to their ability, and beyond their ability, they gave of their own accord, begging us with much urging for the favor of participation in the support of the saints, and this, not as we had expected, but they first gave themselves to the Lord and to us by the will of God. So we urged Titus that as he had previously made a beginning, so he would also complete in you this gracious work as well.

But just as you abound in everything, in faith and utterance and knowledge and in all earnestness and in the love we inspired in you, see that you abound in this gracious work also. I am not speaking this as a command, but as proving through the earnestness of others the sincerity of your love also. For you know the grace of our Lord Jesus Christ, that though He was rich, yet for your sake He became poor, so that you through His poverty might become rich. I give my opinion in this matter, for this is to your advantage, who were the first to begin a year ago not only to do this, but also to desire to do it. But now finish doing it also, so that just as there was the readiness to desire it, so there may be also the completion of it by your ability.

2 Corinthians 8:1-11

CHAPTER TWO

You Know the Grace of Our Lord Jesus Christ

Why give? What would motivate you to take that which is of value to you and hand it to someone else? Certainly no natural instinct. Our visceral inclination is like that of the snapping turtle. We say, "It's *mine*. I *need* it."

This book answers the "why give?" question in several ways. Further down the path, we will be challenged and motivated by Paul's radical view of surplus, his unflagging trust in God's provision, and his insight into generosity's outcomes. But here at the beginning of our trek, Paul exposes us to the primary motivation for fearless generosity: God's grace.

If you think that you already know about the activity of God's grace in giving, let me challenge you with this thought: what we know is reflected in what we do. That being the criterion, how deep is your knowledge?

Beyond Their Ability

When Paul arrived in Macedonia to visit the churches of Philippi, Thessalonica, and Berea, he surely felt some trepidation about broaching the subject of the collection for Jerusalem because the Macedonians were struggling themselves. They were experiencing what Paul calls "deep poverty" and "a great ordeal of affliction."

It may be that the Macedonians felt the sting of maltreatment because of their confession of Jesus. Such abuse came to Paul himself in all three of these Macedonian towns when he first brought them the gospel, especially from the hand of Jewish radicals (you might remember that a Jewish-instigated riot drove Paul out of Thessalonica; Acts 17:5). This maltreatment may have been the cause of their economic difficulty. We cannot be sure. Regardless, "affliction" and "poverty" were the words that came to Paul's mind when he reached them. If times were tough in Jerusalem and the rest of Judea, they were also tough in Macedonia.

That is why Paul did not have high expectations for their generosity. In fact, he may not have even asked them to give, which makes what happened next all the more surprising.

Paul explains that in the barren soil of the Macedonians' poverty and affliction, a vibrant surplus of joy was thriving, which caused an extraordinary demonstration of generosity to spring up. In an ironic wordplay, Paul is able to say that their "*poverty*" overflowed in a "*wealth* of liberality."

It was remarkable enough that the Macedonians gave at all, given that Paul may not have even asked them to. They actually had to *beg him* for the privilege of joining in. We can imagine Paul, maybe a bit distressed by the gift they were offering, countering, "Look, are you sure?" Yes, they were sure. It was their own idea ("of their own accord"); they wanted to do it. To them, it was a privilege.

But even more remarkable was the *extent* of their giving.

> For I testify that according to their ability, and beyond their ability . . . they gave . . . (2 Corinthians 8:3)

It would have been reasonable, and even sacrificial, for them to contribute a portion of whatever surplus some might have had, however small. This would have been something they were "able" to do. Yet the Macedonians dug deeper. Like the widow that Jesus observed in the temple treasury, they gave even out of what they had to live on—that is, "beyond their ability." Their sacrifice was moving to Paul and provided a challenging example for the Corinthians, whose turn to finalize their contribution was soon to come. As we will see, Paul did not necessarily expect them to attain this extreme level of generosity, but he begins here because it was a motivating revelation of God's grace.

"God's grace"—we should pause here to take careful note of that terminology, since it is one of several key terms throughout the whole passage. Did you notice this word when Paul began his account of the Macedonians' giving?

. . . we wish to make known to you the grace of God
which has been given in the churches of Macedonia . . .
(2 Corinthians 8:1)

We might have expected something more direct like, "We
want to tell you about the Macedonians' generosity," or
"We want to fill you in on how the Macedonians gave." But
no, he begins in a very different place. He wants to make
known to them the grace of God which has been *given* to the
Macedonians. Paul knows that the Macedonians' generosity
did not begin with them, but with God. God was the one who
worked in them, filling them with the joy and inspiration to
give despite their circumstances. It was *his* grace, given first
of all to them, which enabled them to engage in their own
"act of grace" toward others (note how Paul uses the word
"grace," translated "gracious work," to describe the act of
giving to the collection throughout the passage). In other
words, God was the truly generous one and only because of
him did the Macedonians have the joy and the readiness to
be generous themselves. This is a very important concept
we will return to later.

Finish What You Started!

The startling act of the Macedonians was one reason why
Paul urged Titus, his traveling companion and ministry
helper, to go on ahead of him to Corinth, carrying this letter. It
turns out that this was not the first time the Corinthians had
heard about the collection for the Judean churches. A year
earlier, Titus had been in Corinth and explained the situation
(see 8:6, "he had previously made a beginning"). How did the
Corinthians react? Eagerly. They were excited; they wanted to

join in. In fact, they may have even begun to set aside money right then.

> . . . [you] who were the first to begin a year ago not only to do this, but also to desire to do it. (2 Corinthians 8:10)

They were in all the way. And they knew that Paul would return again in a year or so to carry the money to Jerusalem.

Now the year had passed and Paul was soon to be on his way to Corinth. Before coming, he sent Titus ahead with this letter so that he would "complete in you this gracious work." Paul must have been a little worried. Maybe he sensed that their eagerness was waning. Maybe he thought that they would be tempted not to contribute after all, or not as generously as they had promised. And while he is careful to say that he is only giving his opinion about the matter and not a command, he encourages them, with no tip-toeing around the topic, to "finish doing it" (8:11). They have an overflowing surplus of many wonderful characteristics—such as faith, knowledge, and love (8:7)—but he urges them to overflow in generosity as well.

Though He Was Rich, He Became Poor

At this point, Paul places another inspiring illustration alongside the example of the Macedonians. This time it is the example of Jesus himself—his generous emptying of himself to become human for the salvation of humanity. The poetic way that Paul expresses this is memorable and impactful. It is an instance of what scholars call a *chiasm* [pronounced, KAI-az-um], which means that the lines are

21

grouped in such a way that the first and last lines parallel each other and the inner two lines parallel each other.

For you know the grace of our Lord Jesus Christ

      that though he was **rich**
                 he became **poor**
    [so you]   through his **poverty**
      might become **rich**

What Paul says is interesting for two reasons. First, he expresses Jesus' redemptive action in economic terms. Jesus was "rich" but for their sake became "poor." Paul is not describing what was in Jesus' bank account. Jesus was rich, not in material wealth, but because he had the status, rights, and joys of being God. Yet he gave up these things to become a human, becoming inextricably one with our world of pains, limitations, humiliations, and sorrows, even to the extreme of crucifixion. He came to live, and die, in our slum so that we might be freed from the cycle of poverty to live a new life outside of it. There are many images Paul could have drawn on to describe the incarnation, such as slavery and freedom or death and life, but he chooses this image of poverty and wealth because it was exactly in this area that the Corinthians needed inspiration.

Second, Paul once again employs that word "grace" to describe what Jesus did. Having just encouraged them to excel in the "gracious work" (literally "grace"), namely giving to the collection, he reminds them, "For you know the grace of our Lord Jesus Christ." In other words, he expects that the inspiration, perhaps the *primary* inspiration, for their sacrificial generosity would be the generosity of Jesus himself. And not just the generosity of Jesus expressed toward anybody—an inspiring story and example to emulate—but the generosity of Jesus expressed toward *them*. When they were in deep need, Jesus put aside his riches in order to enrich *them*. The grace of God that they had become partakers of was to be the foundation of their own grace toward others.

The Candlesticks Too

In a famous sequence from Victor Hugo's *Les Miserables*, the recently-released convict Jean Valjean finds that he is abused and ignored by all members of society because of his previous criminal record. This, along with years of life in the chain gangs, has birthed in him smoldering anger and a harsh philosophy of self-preservation.

On a stormy night he is unexpectedly invited indoors by a priest, who feeds him and gives him a bed to sleep in. Still full of anger and distrust, Valjean gets up while it is dark, steals the priest's valuable silver forks and spoons, and runs away. That morning the priest hears someone pounding on the door. The village police have caught Valjean and have come to return the silverware. Valjean is sure to be destined for many more years of life as a convict in the chain gangs. The policemen claim that Valjean had tried to lie to them by telling them that the silverware was a gift. Yet, remarkably, the priest corroborates the story. He says to the bewildered Valjean in front of the policemen,

I gave you the candlesticks too, which are of silver like the rest, and for which you can certainly get two hundred francs. Why did you not carry them away with your forks and spoons?

Valjean can barely understand what is happening. As the priest presses the candlesticks into his hand, he says (or sings in the musical adaptation), "I have bought your soul for God." And indeed, Valjean's life was transformed. Throughout the rest of the story, he is marked by love and generosity even toward the most unworthy people—even toward the man who wishes to see him ruined and taken back to prison.

Apprehension of grace makes us people of grace. We are compelled to replicate the grace shown to us. Do not think lightly of God's work in inspiring obedience. Just as Valjean was transformed by an astonishingly generous act, we who have received God's almost incomprehensible grace cannot be the same. When we meditate on how Jesus entered into our poverty so that we might become rich, our need to preserve ourselves, our way of life, our futures, even the size of our bank accounts, dissolves.

Yet there is more. Our generosity is not only motivated by God's grace toward us; it is itself a product of God's grace working *in* us. When Paul was telling the Corinthians about the Macedonians' generosity, he was actually describing "the grace of God given in the churches of Macedonia"—that is, the grace that God had worked in them to inspire and enable them to give. Surprisingly, it was not ultimately the Macedonians' work; it was God's from the beginning.

Think about this deeply. Even our own generosity is a result of God's grace working in us and through us. It is *his* work. He begins it in our hearts and enables us to carry it through, for his purposes. Knowing this can give us immense confidence and joy. If it is his work, he will take care of us and accomplish what he desires through it.

Why give? Because God is an abundant giver. We have both received his grace and have been made conduits of it, plugged into the coursing electricity of his generosity. So we can be free and fearless givers. It does not depend on us to work out all the figures and plan for all the contingencies. We let his plans run their course while we participate in them with joy.

Questions for Discussion

1. List every reason you can think of to give generously and fearlessly.

2. Do you recall any experience in your own life or the lives of others when a person or group gave "beyond their ability?" What concerns would you have about a relative or friend who decided to go that far in his or her giving?

3. Did you ever have an intense desire to be an especially generous giver? Has that desire waned or increased? For what reasons? Please try to be very honest.

4. What do you think about the concept that giving begins with God? Does it provide any additional impetus for you to give? Explain.

For if the readiness is present, it is acceptable according to what a person has, not according to what he does not have. For this is not for the ease of others and for your affliction, but by way of equality—at this present time your abundance being a supply for their need, so that their abundance also may become a supply for your need, that there may be equality; as it is written, "He who gathered much did not have too much, and he who gathered little had no lack."

2 Corinthians 8:12-15

CHAPTER THREE

By Way of Equality

Many of us live with surplus. We consider it normal (even essential) for our income to surpass what we need for the current week or month. Yet consider that surplus is by definition unneeded, at least for the moment. That is what the word surplus means. What, then, should we do with it?

For most of us, the answer seems obvious. We put it away toward retirement or an emergency fund, invest it, or use it to purchase something that we want. This is what surplus is for. Right?

But *is* it right?

A Question of Equality

Paul has spoken passionately and inspirationally about the generosity of the Macedonians and of Jesus. With both of these examples of God's grace, he hopes to motivate the Corinthians to bring to completion their own generous intentions, which were begun a year before *in their hearts* but now are ready to be finished *by their actions.* Paul is quite clear that his purpose in bringing forward these examples is to inspire them, and even to test them.

> I am not speaking this as a command, but as proving through the earnestness of others the sincerity of your love also. (2 Corinthians 8:8)

The "earnestness of others" here is that of the Macedonians and Jesus. Paul is asking the Corinthians: "Do you have the same love that they do?"

But now Paul feels the need to soften his tone. After all, the Macedonians have given so sacrificially—"beyond their ability"—that Paul wants to assure the Corinthians that he is not actually expecting them to go to the same extreme. The Macedonians dug shockingly deep, even drawing on what they required for themselves, but Paul is only expecting the Corinthians to give what they are able. As long as the same love and eagerness is present in them, their gift will be pleasing to God, even if it is only out of their surplus.

> But now finish doing it also, so that just as there was the readiness to desire it, so there may be also the completion of it by your ability. For if the readiness is present, it is acceptable according to what a person has, not according to what he does not have.
> (2 Corinthians 8:11-12)

Surely Paul would have been thrilled, and moved, to see the Corinthians match the sacrifice of the Macedonians and follow the example of Christ who became poor for our sake. But, he says, the "readiness" is what matters. If that is present, God is pleased with the gift, in proportion to the giver's ability.

Paul is trying to avoid a misunderstanding. The Corinthians may get the impression that he is traveling among Gentile churches urging them to give to the point of poverty and then taking their gifts back across the world to enrich these Jewish people they have never even met. The Corinthian Christians may think that Paul expects them to suffer so that the Judean churches can live extravagantly. But this is not the case at all, as Paul explains.

> For this is not for the ease of others and for your affliction, but by way of equality . . . (2 Corinthians 8:13)

Pause here. Paul is emphatic in this case that he is *not* doing this in order to burden them so that the Judeans can live the easy life. He does not intend for them to exchange their life situations—rich for poor, poor for rich. Rather, he says, it is a question of equality.

One English translation uses the word "fairness" here instead of "equality," but this misses the nuance. Paul is not concerned here with matters of justice. Instead, he sees an opportunity for those who have too much to voluntarily "even out" their resources with those who have too little.

How can such equality be achieved? Paul's answer is: through a thoughtful use of surplus. Consider how he describes the kind of equality he is thinking of.

> . . . at this present time your abundance being a supply for their need, so that their abundance also may become a supply for your need, that there may be equality. (2 Corinthians 8:14)

We could just as well translate the Greek word "abundance" as "surplus," a word which Paul uses in various forms nine times throughout these two chapters. It is the "extra" that is leftover after one's own needs are met. Paul is urging the Corinthians to reconsider the purpose of their surplus. Currently, the situation is imbalanced. While the Corinthians have more than they need, the Judeans have much less than they need—a deficit. We could illustrate the situation like this.

Judeans   Corinthians
■   ■ ■ ■

Let us imagine that two squares represent what is needed to live on. In this case, the Judeans have less than they need (one square) and the Corinthians have more than they need (three squares). What does Paul want to happen? He wants the Corinthians to take the one square that they do not need and give it in order to supply the Judeans' one square deficit. This will create the happy result that both sides will now have two squares, just what they need to live on.

Judeans   Corinthians
■ ■   ■ ■

But this is not the end of the story in Paul's mind. Someday, the situation may be reversed. There may come a time when the Corinthians will be in a difficult spot, with one square, so to speak, and the Judeans will have a surplus. Once again the unequal situation can be remedied if the Judeans will use their "extra" to supply what the Corinthians lack. Paul's big idea is that these churches should pursue equality in times of acute need by using their surplus to remedy the deficits of others. This is not a very complicated idea, but two millennia later it is still challenging to apply with wisdom.

There are two ways that the Corinthians could have approached the possibility of someday being in need. On the one hand, they could have thought, "Here we have more than we need. Let's take the leftover and store it away until we might need it." But Paul suggests an alternate route. He says, "Here you have more than you need. Why not use it to help others who don't have enough? And then someday when you are in need, they may be able to help you." This is a strange and possibly frightening concept. Yet there is something beautiful about it, because it foregrounds others' needs rather than our own.

The Miracle of Manna

Paul concludes his discussion of the principle of equality with a reference to the Old Testament story of the exodus and wilderness wandering. Almost immediately after God had led the Israelites out of slavery in Egypt, they began to grumble about not having enough food. They said that they remembered the meat pots that they ate from in Egypt, and the bread that filled their stomachs. "You have brought us out into this wilderness to kill this whole assembly with hunger," they wailed (Exodus 16:3).

God's response was to provide for them miraculously. Every evening quails would fly in and cover the camp, and every morning the dew would evaporate and leave a white substance on the ground. The Israelites called this substance "manna" (meaning "what is it?" in Hebrew). The most important part of the story for our purposes is when the people began to collect the manna to eat. God instructed each person to gather just what he or she needed for the day, an omer (a unit of measurement) apiece.

> The sons of Israel did so, and some gathered much and some little. When they measured it with an omer, he who had gathered much had no excess, and he who had gathered little had no lack; every man gathered as much as he should eat. (Exodus 16:17-18)

When they brought back what they had gathered, a strange thing happened. Though some people had gathered too much and some too little, each one ended up with exactly an omer when it was measured. God had provided for each person equally. No remaining surpluses, no remaining deficits.

And nothing left over for tomorrow either. When some tried to save for the next day, Exodus tells us that "it bred worms and became foul" (Exodus 16:20). Each person had exactly what was needed, and only what was needed, for the day.

Paul finds in this story a principle for the Corinthians and for us, though with one key difference. The principle is that God still desires some kind of equality among his people. The difference is that now this equality is entirely voluntary. You have a choice for your excess to be the means to fill another's lack.

So Paul's teaching here to the Corinthians, and to us, is both reassuring and alarming. It is reassuring because it shows us that God is pleased with generosity even if it does not reach the extreme level of the Macedonians. Though Jesus did indeed become poor to make others rich (which was even more extreme), and though we may follow his example, we can begin simply with the idea of equality.

And this pursuit of equality is alarming enough because it forces us to think again, and think hard, about how we view surplus. Is it in fact true that God has given us this excess so that we can save it, invest it, or use it for something that we do not truly need? Or could it be that God has given it to us so that we can meet others' needs? Could we be content with just enough for our immediate needs, as God intended the Israelites to be?

An Unending and Holy Tension

Paul does not interact with the ten thousand questions and scenarios playing in your mind at this moment. No doubt they were in the minds of the Corinthians as well. For example, does not Paul talk about rich people being part of the church in some of his letters (e.g. 1 Timothy 6:17-19)? What about the proverb of the ant who stores up provisions for his future (Proverbs 6:6-8)? Is this a principle for the ordering of societies and the governing of nations; does it provide a "right" for the poor, for example (note: I do not think so)? Surely Paul does not mean that all believers and churches should always be at exactly the same economic level, right? What, in other words, is the extent of the application of this text?

I leave you to wrestle with these and many more questions in prayer alongside fellow believers in your family and spiritual community. There is an unending and holy tension that the Spirit places in our lives through such texts wherever they are found in the Bible. The answers are not intended to be easy, and herein lies the danger for the careless Christian. It is the danger of extracting the teeth from the teaching. We are not supposed to be comfortable in a casual camaraderie with surplus. God meant it when he said, "Do not love the world nor the things in the world" (1 John 2:15). The use of money, after all, has always been a litmus test of biblical spirituality.

The sad reality is that such texts pose no tension at all for some. They are satisfied to tip God every week or month and occasionally offer a little change for a need that is presented. But they never really grapple with the call to the compassionate use of their abundance. By applying convenient exceptions at every turn, they end up living as if passages like this never said anything at all. They might as well have not been included in the Scriptures. Such people will die without ever having walked in true biblical generosity.

What About This Idea?

Churches often hold large amounts of surplus. Most would not *say* they have more than they need, but many do in fact have an abundance. Why the surplus?

When my father stepped into leadership of a church in the southern United States, almost every person who had gotten the church into serious debt had left. Those who remained shouldered bond payments amounting to 70-80% of the weekly offerings. Every Friday the bill was due. When this was over, a huge balloon note was looming still. These dear hardworking folks trusted God throughout this ordeal and, amazingly, the entire remaining debt was eventually paid off. However, for years prior to this, the leaders often could not even afford to send a letter to the members, or make necessary repairs to the building, or buy literature.

Nearby was a large church that could have relieved that entire debt by sharing just one week's offering with them. Think of that. My father believes that this generous church might have done this noble thing if it had only seen the potential, but the idea never occurred to them. In fact, it did not really occur to my father until much later—not that he would have asked.

What if your church, even if small, designated a Sunday to share your entire offering with a sister church in need? Think of what this could mean for the kingdom. Think of the growing love between the churches. Think of the powerful display of the gospel that such a gift would be. They would glorify God for such generosity.

Christian families or individuals can do the same. Many of you have more than you need. Could you do something useful for God's kingdom by giving to the needs of others? What about missionaries or Christian workers? What about those who live under the shadow of debt because of foolish decisions made years before. What about elderly brothers and sisters who struggle to get by now that they are past working age? What about that believer who just lost his job? Could it be that God has given you too much so that you can fill their lack?

"I Dare Not Save"

In 1836, George Muller opened his first home for orphans in Bristol, England. The Prussian determined to use his growing orphan work to demonstrate God's faithfulness by simply praying for the money and supplies necessary to support them, without asking anybody for help. Over his lifetime, more than 10,000 orphans were fed, clothed, and taught, through prayer and God's miraculous provision.

But Muller's uncommon perspectives on money touched his personal life as well, especially his use of surplus. One biographer notes something truly remarkable:

> It is known that during his life he received about £93,000 for his personal expenses: of this he gave away over £81,000; at his death his sole estate was valued at about £160, including household furniture.[1]

---

[1] Roger Steer, *George Muller: Delighted in God* (Wheaton: Harold Shaw Publishers, 1975), 327.

In other words, of all that Muller received for personal expenses over the nearly 70 years of ministry, he gave away more than 87 percent. What he kept was only what he needed to live on.

Once, near the end of his life, he was asked, "You never thought of saving for yourself?" Taking out a small purse from his coat pocket, he replied,

> All I am possessed of is in that purse—every penny! Save for *myself*? Never! When money is sent to me for my own use, I pass it on to God . . . I do not regard such gifts as belonging to me; they belong to Him, whose I am and whom I serve. Save for *myself*? I dare not save; it would dishonor my loving, gracious, all-bountiful Father.[2]

Muller was a truly radical thinker about surplus, perhaps too radical for most. His voice comes to us as if from another world; it sounds unrealistic and out of touch. Yet for him, all the common sense of our age is swallowed up in the unfailing faithfulness of a loving, gracious, and all-bountiful Father.

Even I wonder if he is not speaking too strongly. Should we save for ourselves? I do not fully know. I am still wrestling with this question in the various situations of my own life. But at the very least we must ask ourselves: could he be right?

---

[2] Steer, *George Muller*, 309.

Questions for Discussion

1. What do you think of Paul's principle of equality? How do you think it should be applied?

2. Do you think it is irresponsible, or even possible, to live without surplus?

3. Do you agree or disagree with Muller's perspective on this issue? Would you nuance it in some way?

But thanks be to God who puts the same earnestness on your behalf in the heart of Titus. For he not only accepted our appeal, but being himself very earnest, he has gone to you of his own accord. We have sent along with him the brother whose fame in the things of the gospel has spread through all the churches; and not only this, but he has also been appointed by the churches to travel with us in this gracious work, which is being administered by us for the glory of the Lord Himself, and to show our readiness, taking precaution so that no one will discredit us in our administration of this generous gift; for we have regard for what is honorable, not only in the sight of the Lord, but also in the sight of men.

We have sent with them our brother, whom we have often tested and found diligent in many things, but now even more diligent because of his great confidence in you. As for Titus, he is my partner and fellow worker among you; as for our brethren, they are messengers of the churches, a glory to Christ. Therefore openly before the churches, show them the proof of your love and of our reason for boasting about you.

2 Corinthians 8:16-24

CHAPTER FOUR

So That No One Will Discredit Us

Suspicion is a major hindrance to generosity. This is especially so in our day when the unpleasant smell of charlatan preachers taints almost every discussion of Christ and money. "What's the gimmick?" we want to know. "What's in this for him?" We are wary of being duped, especially by professing Christians.

In this section, we will see that integrity, or lack of it, affects generosity. Paul seeks to overcome the suspicions of the Corinthian church in order to free them to give generously. He affirms to them that his motives are pure and that he is administering their gift with the utmost care.

A Breakdown of Trust

Paul's relationship with the Corinthians was sometimes rocky. We know that at some point before writing 2 Corinthians, Paul made a short and painful visit to Corinth (2 Corinthians 2:1-4), which he then followed up with a harsh letter that is now lost to us. He says they were grieved by this letter and that it led them to some measure of repentance (2 Corinthians 7:8-9). It appears that some of the Corinthian Christians began to reject Paul's leadership and became ashamed of his unimpressive physical presence, his teaching style, his poverty, and his life of suffering. This was not the kind of leader they felt they should be taking orders from. Instead, they had become more attracted to certain wealthier and more successful leaders whom Paul sarcastically labels "super-apostles." These men were sowing seeds of doubt among the Corinthian believers about Paul's motives and genuine care for them. The point is this: though things had gotten a little better, there had been a breakdown of trust.

This may help us to understand why Paul expends extra effort here to allay any suspicions about his motives in the collection, or the motives of his fellow-travelers. He wants to assure the Corinthians that they are engaging in this work only for God's glory and with every precaution. The Corinthians should therefore have no reason to withhold from contributing as liberally as they had promised.

Three Men at the Door

If you look closely at this section of 2 Corinthians 8 (verses 16-24), you will notice that it sounds very much like a recommendation letter. Paul is writing to introduce and commend three men to the Corinthians—Titus and two "brothers," as he calls them. When the letter is read, they will have just arrived.

The Corinthians already knew Titus, who had been in Corinth on multiple occasions. We have already learned that Titus was in some way involved a year before in encouraging the Corinthians to contribute to the collection. And now, as we saw in 8:6, Titus is going to Corinth ahead of Paul in order to arrange the collection before Paul arrives. In Paul's words, Titus is coming to "complete" the "gracious work." And along with Titus, Paul sends this letter that we are now reading.

Paul is careful to note that Titus really *wanted* to come. Yes, Paul had asked him to go, but Titus was invested enough in the project and in the Corinthians' wellbeing that he did not really need to be asked. "For he not only accepted our appeal, but being himself very earnest, he has gone to you of his own accord" (8:17). Given the history of relations between them, Paul wants to make absolutely clear to the believers in Corinth that he is not the only one who is concerned that they carry through with their contribution.

But Titus is not traveling alone. With him are two others, "our brothers," as Paul calls them. Unfortunately for us, he neither mentions their names nor where they are from, since they would have already arrived and introduced themselves to the congregation before the letter was read.

We can see that one of these men was well-known among several of the churches.

> We have sent along with him [Titus] the brother whose fame in the things of the gospel has spread through all the churches; and not only this, but he has also been appointed by the churches to travel with us in this gracious work . . . (2 Corinthians 8:18)

This may or may not be hyperbole. Paul may mean that he was famous to *all* the existing churches of the time, or simply that he had a good reputation among the congregations of his region—either Macedonia, Asia, or maybe Galatia—which led those churches to appoint him as a representative to travel with Paul as he gathered the collection.

Along with Titus and this famed brother was another believer. This man, like the first, was traveling as a representative of the churches. "They are messengers of the churches," Paul says. Yet this man seems to be more well-known to Paul personally. His affirmation that they had often tested him and found him diligent may indicate that Paul had partnered with him in ministry at times.

> We have sent with them our brother, whom we have often tested and found diligent in many things, but now even more diligent because of his great confidence in you. (2 Corinthians 8:22)

In the case of each of the three men, Paul is working hard to establish their credibility to the Corinthians. He wants to remove from them any hint of suspicion which might provide a weak excuse that would hinder the Corinthian believers' generosity.

> As for Titus, he is my partner and fellow worker among you; as for our brethren, they are messengers of the churches, a glory to Christ. (2 Corinthians 8:23)

The Danger of Being Discredited

This concern for credibility is in keeping with the overall purpose of the delegation. Paul has tried his best to build a strategic entourage around him who could be involved in the collection and delivery of this gift to Jerusalem. This group is made up of representatives of various churches as well as some of Paul's own ministry companions, such as Titus. Later, in Acts 20, when he was finally about to set off for Jerusalem from Corinth, we find out that he was accompanied by no less than seven men, whom Luke lists by region.

> And he was accompanied by
> Sopater of Berea, the son of Pyrrhus
> and by Aristarchus and Secundus of the
> Thessalonians
> and Gaius of Derbe and Timothy
> and Tychicus and Trophimus of Asia
> (Acts 20:3-6)

The first three (Sopater, Aristarchus, and Secundus) were from the Macedonian region, Gaius and Timothy were from Galatia, and Tychicus and Trophimus were from the province of Asia (where Ephesus was). This represents well the regions where Paul planted churches. And still there were more. Luke, for one, includes himself in the company as the author of Acts (see the "us" in Acts 20:5). We also know that Paul originally wanted someone from Corinth to come along once their gift had been finalized (1 Corinthians 16:3-4). Furthermore, some of Paul's long-term assistants such as

Titus were involved at certain points in the process, as we have noted.

From this perspective, it all begins to look like a massive undertaking, involving months of travel for over 10 people. Why so much effort? In the first place was the danger and difficulty of sending money in the ancient world. Without electronic transfer or other modern conveniences, money and goods had to be carried from place to place, risking highway robbery and shipwreck, at the very least. Anything of value would need to be sent with a band of trusted associates.

For Paul, beyond the dangers of travel loomed the even greater danger of being discredited. If Paul were to carry the gift alone or with only one or two companions, there would be many opportunities for foul play. After all, no one in Jerusalem knew how much money they should expect to receive. Paul could easily have helped himself to some along the way. So, to guard against any accusations of this type, he made sure to involve many people in the process, including delegates from each of the churches who contributed.

> . . . which is being administered by us for the glory of the Lord Himself, and to show our readiness, taking precaution so that no one will discredit us in our administration of this generous gift; for we have regard for what is honorable, not only in the sight of the Lord, but also in the sight of men. (2 Corinthians 8:20)

Here Paul gives one more assurance about his own motives. Why is he so interested in this collection in the first place?

For personal gain? Not at all. This act of grace is being administered by us, he says, "for the glory of the Lord Himself, and to show our readiness" (8:19). He was in it for Jesus' glory and to demonstrate his eagerness to help in time of need.

Some may have been quick to misinterpret what Paul was trying to accomplish. By taking this gift to Jerusalem, he could certainly elevate his status with the Jewish church there. And some in Corinth, who were tempted to mistrust Paul and reject his leadership, could have convinced themselves of this narrative and propagated it to others. "He's using us to get approval from the mother church!" Or perhaps they would believe that he had plans to gain by shifty handling of the funds.

But Paul repudiates this interpretation of the project and takes every precaution so that no such accusation could ever stand. The Corinthians therefore have no reason to hold back as these delegates arrive. Their opportunity has come to put their own love and eagerness to help on display openly, in front of these representatives of the churches.

> Therefore openly before the churches, show them the proof of your love and of our reason for boasting about you. (2 Corinthians 8:24)

Integrity Affects Generosity

This book is written to encourage you to be generous. It parallels Paul's purpose in writing 2 Corinthians 8-9. He wrote to urge the Corinthians to give, accumulating reasons to motivate their generosity. In the section we have just examined he provides yet another reason, saying, in effect, "Give because you do not have to be suspicious of my motives or my administration of this collection."

While this is extremely important in Paul's historically-located interaction with the Corinthian church, it leaves us without a direct application for givers today. We cannot casually take Paul's injunction for ourselves: "Let's give to the collection for Jerusalem, because Paul is doing it for the right reasons!" We missed that train by millennia.

There may be an application concerning the integrity of churches and ministries who *receive* money to channel into God's kingdom work, but neither the thrust of Paul's argument nor the emphasis of this book leads us to develop it further here.

As responsible Bible readers then we must be content with a simple statement: integrity affects generosity. Paul believed that generosity would flourish in this case if he would emphasize his integrity and break down any suspicions the Corinthians might have harbored.

Questions for Discussion

1. Do you have any stories or observations about lack of financial integrity in the religious world today?

2. What do you recall are the various ways that Paul seeks to have integrity in the collection for Jerusalem?

3. Why do I think that we should be reticent to make a direct application of this section? Do you agree?

4. Moving beyond application of this particular text, in what ways do you think "integrity affects generosity"?

5. In what ways does your church or the ministries you support ensure financial integrity?

For it is superfluous for me to write to you about this ministry to the saints; for I know your readiness, of which I boast about you to the Macedonians, namely, that Achaia has been prepared since last year, and your zeal has stirred up most of them. But I have sent the brethren, in order that our boasting about you may not be made empty in this case, so that, as I was saying, you may be prepared; otherwise if any Macedonians come with me and find you unprepared, we—not to speak of you—will be put to shame by this confidence. So I thought it necessary to urge the brethren that they would go on ahead to you and arrange beforehand your previously promised bountiful gift, so that the same would be ready as a bountiful gift and not affected by covetousness.

Now this I say, he who sows sparingly will also reap sparingly, and he who sows bountifully will also reap bountifully. Each one must do just as he has purposed in his heart, not grudgingly or under compulsion, for God loves a cheerful giver.

2 Corinthians 9:1-7

CHAPTER FIVE

Not Grudgingly or Under Compulsion

True generosity emerges from an attitude of the heart. It comes from an eager disposition to bless others, from a heart that thrills at the prospect of meeting a need. It arises in a person who knows that, strangely, being generous makes you happy. This kind of person is not begrudging, but is like Ebenezer Scrooge, who, after buying a prize turkey twice the size of Tiny Tim on Christmas morning, could barely even shave for all his chuckling, excited shaking, and dancing. This is the kind of giver God loves—the cheerful giver. That is why Paul goes to great effort to encourage the Corinthians, not only to give, but to give with joy.

Creeping Covetousness

We have seen one reason why Paul involved the three-man delegation of Titus and the two "brothers." He is concerned, he says, not to be discredited in the administration of the gift for Jerusalem. He is also very careful to draw attention to the well-attested character of these men, recommending them heartily. In all of this, he wants the Corinthian believers to know that he and these delegates have no other motive than to collect and deliver this gift for God's own glory. Despite the previous breakdown of trust between them, the Corinthian Christians are to believe in Paul, receive these delegates, and step up to fulfill their previous promise.

Yet a question remains. Why did Paul send this delegation *ahead of him*? He could have easily brought them with him later. Why does he send them while he himself stays back in Macedonia, promising to come soon?

The text reveals two answers to this puzzle. The first is actually rather humorous. Paul writes:

> For it is superfluous for me to write to you about this ministry to the saints; for I know your readiness . . .
> (2 Corinthians 9:1-2a)

Paul is a little worried, though he is unwilling to admit it directly. He writes like a mother who tells her son to clean up his room in preparation for the guests who are coming for dinner. "Did you clean up your room?" she asks. "Yes," comes the reply. "Okay, I believe you," she says as she goes to check on it herself. Or, put another way, Paul's words sound a little like this: "Oh I'm quite confident that you're going to do it . . . I mean, you *are* going to do it, right?"

What is more important is that Paul has even sung the praises of their generosity to the Macedonians.

. . . for I know your readiness, of which I boast about you to the Macedonians, namely, that Achaia [the region which includes Corinth] has been prepared since last year, and your zeal has stirred up most of them. (2 Corinthians 9:1-2)

Things are now in a slightly awkward position. The Corinthians' commitment to generosity, which they affirmed a year before, was a stimulant to the Macedonians. Even though he may not have asked them to give, Paul's report about the Corinthians' zeal stirred them up so much that they begged him for the opportunity to contribute as well. And then they did give, as we have seen, far beyond their ability.

But now Paul is nervous that the Corinthians' fervor, which was so inspiring to the Macedonians, is down to a smolder. What would happen now if Paul were to show up unannounced in Corinth, with some Macedonians along with him, only to find that the Corinthians were not really as generous as he had said they were? Embarrassment all around.

But I have sent the brethren, in order that our boasting about you may not be made empty in this case, so that, as I was saying, you may be prepared; otherwise if any Macedonians come with me and find you unprepared, we—not to speak of you—will be put to shame by this confidence. (2 Corinthians 9:3-4)

We have probably all experienced a similar feeling. Perhaps you have highly recommended a restaurant and taken your friend there, only to find that the food served that day is actually rather bad. This, then, is the first reason that Paul sends this delegation on ahead of him. He wants them to be prepared to live up to the commitment that inspired the Macedonians so that, when he and some Macedonians finally do come, neither he nor they will be put to shame.

But there is a second reason, which speaks to our lives more directly. Paul sends these three men ahead of him because he is concerned not only that the Corinthian believers *would* give, but also about *how* they would give. This was about their attitude.

> So I thought it necessary to urge the brethren that they would go on ahead to you and arrange beforehand your previously promised bountiful gift, so that the same would be ready as a bountiful gift and not affected by covetousness. (2 Corinthians 9:5)

Paul apparently felt that if he were to arrive unexpectedly along with some Macedonians, this could seriously affect the attitude with which they gave. It is important that we note here that the original wording of the phrase translated as "bountiful gift" is more literally "blessing," or "gift of blessing." The translators are not wrong to render it as they do, but the original word strengthens a nuance that we might otherwise miss. Yes, Paul was hopeful that they would give and give bountifully, as they had promised, but it was as important to him that they would give with a particular heart attitude. It was to be a "bountiful gift," but also a "gift of *blessing*"—that is, given with the real intention of blessing the recipients.

The alternative to this bountiful gift of blessing would be a gift "affected by covetousness." Covetousness is a biblical word that describes selfish desire, usually for possessions. What is fascinating is that such desire can even creep into generosity. The Corinthian believers were not tempted to desire *someone else's* wealth, but were tempted to hold on to *their own* wealth for themselves. The allure of other, self-centered uses of their surplus could erode their original selfless intention. A child may walk into a store with the intention of buying a birthday gift for his mother, but rethink his altruistic plan when confronted with the rows of plastic toys.

We cannot be entirely sure how this might have manifested itself in the Corinthians' situation. Was Paul afraid that they had not been setting aside money for the gift as he had instructed? Perhaps he sent the delegation ahead so that they would have enough time to put the gift together before he arrived. Or maybe he was worried that they might, if surprised by his arrival, second-guess the amount they had set aside and keep some back. In either case, Paul's fear was for their hearts—that what had been originally conceived as an eager and generous gift would become infected by stinginess and selfishness.

This is then the second reason that Paul sent the delegation on ahead. He wanted them to have time to work these things out in their hearts, so that the gift would be given bountifully and with hearts full of the desire to bless others.

The Attitude Behind It

Before leaving this theme, Paul appeals to an agricultural metaphor. Just like a farmer can only expect a large crop if he plants a large quantity of seed, so these believers should not expect a great amount of produce from their generosity if they give sparsely because of selfishness in their hearts.

> Now this I say, he who sows sparingly will also reap sparingly, and he who sows bountifully will also reap bountifully. (2 Corinthians 9:6)

In other words, though some good results may come from a stingy gift, bountiful blessing in their lives and the lives of those who receive it will only come if they contribute lavishly and intentionally. We will discuss what *kind* of blessing later.

Paul sharpens his exhortation to a point in verse 7. He wants each of them to give just as they had previously committed in their hearts to give a year before. Their hearts had been pure at the beginning and now he wants them to follow through with the same attitude they had at first.

> Each one must do just as he has purposed in his heart, not grudgingly or under compulsion, for God loves a cheerful giver. (2 Corinthians 9:7)

As we have seen, Paul *is* concerned with how much the Corinthians give. But he is as much concerned with the attitude that accompanies their giving. Paul has already said that they should not be affected by covetousness—that is, they should not hold back with a grasping attitude. In this verse, he adds two other possible attitudes: (1) "not grudgingly" or (2) "under compulsion."

To give "grudgingly" is to give with a sense of regret.

Begrudging giving hides a secret selfish wish that you had never actually given at all, or that you had not given so much. Giving "under compulsion" carries the sense that someone is forcing you to give. On your own, you would not have done it. The root of both attitudes is selfishness; you are more focused on how your giving affects *you* than how it affects the one to whom you are giving. Paul is afraid that one or both of these selfish attitudes could infiltrate the Corinthians' generosity.

Cheerfulness is that characteristic Paul most wants to see. He urges the Corinthian Christians to replace any reluctance or sense of obligation with real joy. When blessing others becomes the focus, giving is not an obligation but a delight. It is not a task to be avoided, but an opportunity to be seized. The delighted giver is the kind of giver God loves. It is, in fact, the kind of giver God is himself.

A Teenager's Joyful Generosity

An itinerant teacher tells this story:

> Once, when I was speaking to a church in Texas, a teenage boy followed me around after the church meetings. He seemed very interested in what the Lord was showing him and wanted to learn as much as he could from our relationship that could help him grow. I really appreciated that and felt God was doing something special in his life. He came from a good family who also loved Christ.

On the final night the father asked if the family could take me out to breakfast before I left town the next morning. I consented.

We had a good meal together at a restaurant. Then the father said that his son wanted to give me something. He handed me an envelope with $200 in it. The father told me that his son, who was sitting there with us, felt compelled to give this to me.

The father told me that the teenager had been very interested in buying a used computer. So he had arranged to collect the garbage of the neighbors in the rural area where they lived, receiving a little from each family weekly over the year. This had resulted in the $200 I had been handed. Despite his original intentions, the young man's joy and enthusiasm in blessing me with this sacrificial gift was even greater than the potential value of buying a computer.

"I surely can't take this money," I thought. But then the Lord brought to my mind that I should not despise the joy that had generated his giving, and that this joy was more important than the money. I had known that joy myself and found there was none other like it. So I took the money that represented such patient labor and hope with a profound sense that I had experienced something holy and pleasing to God.

I received word later that someone in the church gave the boy a new computer.

Questions for Discussion

1. Have you or someone close to you had a memorable experience of joyful giving? If you are willing, relate it for the encouragement of others, either generally or in specifics.

2. We all face the temptation of covetousness. What are some ways it shows up in your own life? Have you seen it affect your generosity?

3. Why would God care about your attitude in giving? If your giving helps someone else, is it not still a good thing, even if it is done begrudgingly or out of compulsion?

And God is able to make all grace abound to you, so that always having all sufficiency in everything, you may have an abundance for every good deed; as it is written,

"He scattered abroad, he gave to the poor,
His righteousness endures forever."

Now He who supplies seed to the sower and bread for food will supply and multiply your seed for sowing and increase the harvest of your righteousness; you will be enriched in everything for all liberality, which through us is producing thanksgiving to God.

2 Corinthians 9:8-11

CHAPTER SIX

Bread for Food, Seed for Sowing

Here is one of our greatest fears: that our giving will deplete the resources we need for ourselves. Some may ask: "If I give this away, will I have enough to pay next month's rent?" Others wonder: "What if my car breaks down?" Still others: "What will happen to my retirement portfolio if I channel this money to some other purpose?"

The Corinthian Christians must have had similar worries; living in antiquity did not protect them from these basic human fears. So in this section, Paul provides them and us with some of the most encouraging and counter-intuitive promises about generosity in the whole Bible. If we truly believe them, our fear will turn to joyful confidence that our God can indeed provide for us, not in spite of our giving, but because of it.

A Principle and Promise

Paul begins by outlining a principle in verse 7, which he develops in the rest of the section.

> And God is able to make all grace abound to you, so that always having all sufficiency in everything, you may have an abundance for every good deed. (2 Corinthians 9:7)

Notice the two elements of Paul's encouragement. First, if the Corinthians were worried about their own needs, Paul tells them that God is able to give them "all sufficiency in everything." They will have *enough* for their own needs. Second, beyond this, God can also provide them "an abundance for every good deed." That is, they will have a *surplus* to give away. And so, the principle for the Corinthians and for us is this: God is able to give you enough for your own needs *and* a surplus to give away.

This is an incredible possibility. And if we are going to have the same sort of confidence that Paul had, we must begin by adjusting our view of God. In this verse, who is the one who is generous? It is true that the Corinthians are to be givers, deploying their abundance in good deeds. But really, they are recipients first of all. God is the one who gives them both the supply for their own needs and the abundance to use for others. He is, first and foremost, the abundant giver, out of the overflow of his grace.

It is just as we saw in the beginning of the book. Even the Macedonians' giving was ultimately an operation of the generous grace of God within them ("we wish to make known to you the grace of God which has been given in the churches of Macedonia"). Paul then urges the Corinthians to give based on the lavish display of Christ's grace toward them. "You know the grace of our Lord Jesus Christ," he says. And now once again in chapter 9, it is God's grace that initiates and supplies the Corinthians' generosity. "God is able to make all grace abound to you . . ." God is the one who is generous; we join him in his project.

Whose Righteousness Endures Forever?

At this point, Paul quotes from Psalm 112:9 to illustrate and support his claim that God can both supply the Corinthians' needs and fuel their giving. Stay alert here. We are going to dive quite deep in order to understand how this verse is working in context.

> . . . as it is written, "He scattered abroad, he gave to the poor, His righteousness endures forever."
> (2 Corinthians 9:9)

We may be quick to make a basic error about this quote. It sounds very much as if God is the subject of the sentence. "[God] scattered abroad, [God] gave to the poor, [God's] righteousness endures forever." But when we open our Bibles to Psalm 112 and examine the verse in context, we are surprised to find that the subject is not God, but a righteous person who fears God. The psalm begins with "How blessed is the man who fears the Lord" and proceeds to describe what this man is like and how he prospers.

So then, this is about the generosity of the person who fears the Lord. But, while this idea fits the general theme of generosity that Paul is discussing, we must ask if Paul has in mind a more focused purpose for the quote. It certainly sounds as if he is inserting the quote in order to support his claim in the previous verse about God's supply. Pay attention to how it flows: "God is able to make all grace abound to you . . . *as it is written*, 'He scattered abroad, he gave to the poor . . .'" If the quote from Psalm 112 is about a God-fearing person's righteousness, how does it back up what Paul is asserting about God's ability to provide?

A closer look at Psalm 112 reveals another surprise. Psalm 112 is actually a twin to the psalm right before it, Psalm 111. The parallels are impossible to miss. Here are the two psalms side by side with a couple of the more obvious connections underlined. I recommend that you read them carefully. You will understand why in a moment.

Psalm 111

¹ Praise the LORD!
I will give thanks to the LORD with all my heart,
In the company of the upright and in the assembly.
² Great are the works of the LORD;
They are studied by all who delight in them.
³ Splendid and majestic is His work,
And His righteousness endures forever.
⁴ He has made His wonders to be remembered;
The LORD is gracious and compassionate.
⁵ He has given food to those who fear Him;
He will remember His covenant forever.

⁶ He has made known to His people the power of His works,
In giving them the heritage of the nations.
⁷ The works of His hands are truth and justice;
All His precepts are sure.
⁸ They are upheld forever and ever;
They are performed in truth and uprightness.
⁹ He has sent redemption to His people;
He has ordained His covenant forever;
Holy and awesome is His name.
¹⁰ The fear of the LORD is the beginning of wisdom;
A good understanding have all those who do His
commandments;
His praise endures forever.

Psalm 112

¹ Praise the LORD!
How blessed is the man who fears the LORD,
Who greatly delights in His commandments.
² His descendants will be mighty on earth;
The generation of the upright will be blessed.
³ Wealth and riches are in his house,
And his righteousness endures forever.
⁴ Light arises in the darkness for the upright;
He is gracious and compassionate and righteous.
⁵ It is well with the man who is gracious and lends;
He will maintain his cause in judgment.
⁶ For he will never be shaken;
The righteous will be remembered forever.
⁷ He will not fear evil tidings;
His heart is steadfast, trusting in the LORD.
⁸ His heart is upheld, he will not fear,

Until he looks with satisfaction on his adversaries.
⁹ He has given freely to the poor,
<u>His righteousness endures forever;</u>
His horn will be exalted in honor.
¹⁰ The wicked will see it and be vexed,
He will gnash his teeth and melt away;
The desire of the wicked will perish.

The basic thing to see is that the first psalm (111) is about
God—his character and acts; the second psalm (112) is
about *the person who fears God*—his character and acts. By
weaving the parallels together, the writer or writers of these
psalms are intentionally saying that a God-fearing person
bears the same character traits and imitates the same
acts as God himself. Just as God displayed his grace and
generosity toward the Israelites by redeeming them from
slavery in Egypt, feeding them in the wilderness, and leading
them to an inheritance in the promised land, so the person
who fears God displays grace and generosity in taking up
the cause of the disadvantaged and giving to the poor.
Amazingly, even the covenantally-charged description of
God as "gracious and compassionate" (see Exodus 34:6) is
applied to the righteous person as well.

But for our purposes, the most important parallel is the
sentence "his righteousness endures forever." This is said
both of God in 111:3 and twice of the righteous person in
112:3 and 112:9. What does this mean?

Typically, we think of righteousness in one of two categories:
(1) as a status of "not guilty" heard in a courtroom or similar
setting (he is declared righteous), or (2) as an approximate

synonym for holiness or piety ("she's a righteous girl"—i.e. a godly girl, devoted to God). But here in these psalms, and commonly in the Old Testament, righteousness has a different nuance. The righteous person is someone who upholds right relationships with those around him. He "does right by" others, seeking to treat them with respect and equality as God's image in the world. Often this manifests itself in that person's concern for the poor or socially disadvantaged, as we see in this psalm. "He is gracious and compassionate," he is "gracious and lends," "He has given freely to the poor."

By acting in these ways, the righteous person acts like God. God also seeks to "do right by" his creatures, especially those with whom he has uniquely covenanted. He upholds their cause, treats them as valuable, generously provides for them, and always keeps his promises to them. Note how the psalmist communicates these ideas in Psalm 111: "The Lord is gracious and compassionate," "He has given food to those who fear Him," "He will remember His covenant forever," "He has sent redemption to His people."

We have to understand Paul's quotation of "his righteousness endures forever" in this context. What the psalm writer is telling his readers is that God's commitment to treat them well as members of his covenant will never wane. His righteous acts toward them will keep going on and on. In a similar way, the person who imitates God described in Psalm 112 will not pull back in his commitment to treat others with generosity and respect. As with God, his righteous acts will go on and on. This is what it means that "his righteousness endures forever."

But we are left with a paradox. If this person's delight in the Lord's ways leads him to continual generous acts of righteousness toward others, how will he be able to continue these acts without his resources being depleted? Yes, he may have "wealth and riches" (112:3) in his house, but if he scatters abroad and gives to the poor, will not that wealth run out? Not at all, says the psalmist. His righteous acts will continue forever.

I believe that Paul is picking up on this tension in the psalm. He is dealing with that same objection in the Corinthians' thinking. If we act out of abundant generosity, how will we have what we need for ourselves, let alone more to give away later? Paul's answer: if we will pattern our lives after God in righteous generosity toward others, we will never lack God's supply, both for our needs *and* for continuing acts of liberality. Even when we open our hands to scatter our resources abroad and give to the poor, God will restock our resources (our "wealth and riches") so that our righteous deeds can go on and on.

Seed to the Sower

Taking up farming imagery again, Paul restates his principle in verse 10.

> Now He who supplies seed to the sower and bread
> for food will supply and multiply your seed for sowing
> and increase the harvest of your righteousness . . .
> (2 Corinthians 9:10)

Here Paul subtly draws on a phrase from Isaiah 55:10, which compares God's decree (that the Jews will return from exile) to the rainfall which waters the ground and which in turn "gives seed to the sower and bread to the eater." Paul alludes to this phrase to illustrate the two-part principle that he mentioned earlier when he said,

> And God is able to make all grace abound to you, so that always having all sufficiency in everything, you may have an abundance for every good deed. (2 Corinthians 9:7)

The fact that God gives bread for food seems to parallel what Paul has said about God supplying their needs ("having all sufficiency in everything"). And the idea that God supplies seed to the sower seems to parallel what he has said about God providing a surplus to give away ("you may have an abundance for every good deed").

In other words, joining God's generous project is like working with him as if he is a farm supplier. In this setup, enough grain is provided for your sustenance (there is ample "bread for food") *and* seed is also provided for planting.

But now comes the truly remarkable reality. Not only will you be provided with enough seed for planting, your seed for planting will be *multiplied*. For every one bag of seed you go out to plant, there will be more bags waiting to be planted. In other words, the more you give, the more you will *have* to give.

This is no "prosperity gospel." Yes, it is true that the Lord may multiply our seed as we plant it (give it away), but note carefully what the multiplication is for: "he will supply and multiply your seed *for sowing.*" This is not surplus to use on ourselves. No, we continue to eat the bread that the Lord provides for our food. The surplus is for planting. If we give, God will allow us to give more.

John Wesley was known for saying that what should rise is not the Christian's standard of living, but his standard of giving. Wesley backed up this perspective by deciding early in his life that he would live on no more than 30 British pounds a year, approximately his income at the time. He stayed true to this commitment even when his income had grown to 1400 pounds per year.[1]

The end result of this sowing is a harvest: "the harvest of your righteousness," as Paul calls it. If we remember our discussion of the quote from Psalm 112 in verse 9 ("his righteousness endures forever"), it is not hard to see what Paul is communicating here. The Corinthians' righteousness is the righteous action they are to undertake in giving to the poor in Jerusalem, seeking to honor them and care for them as God's creatures and fellow believers. Paul says that God will not only make this generosity possible, he will maximize the effects of it as well. We might paraphrase it like this: "He will increase the good results that come from your righteous action." What kind of good results might come is something we will discuss in the next chapter.

---

[1] Charles Edward White, "Four Lessons on Money from One of the World's Richest Preachers" *Christian History* 19 (summer 1988): 20-25.

The final verse of this section, verse 11, is a wonderful summary of the whole. Consider it carefully and notice how it restates the major principle of this chapter: God is able to give you enough for your own needs and grow a surplus to give away.

> You will be enriched in everything for all liberality, which through us is producing thanksgiving to God.
> (2 Corinthians 9:11)

The Royal Way

"Enriched in everything for all liberality"—what a promise!

Andrew van der Bijl, known as Brother Andrew in his fascinating book *God's Smuggler*, experienced the truth of this principle many times over. When speaking of the surety of God's plentiful provision, he would use the phrase "the Royal Way," communicating that God would always be abundantly generous to his people as a king who loves his subjects. He did not mean that God's followers would live extravagantly (as his own lifestyle showed), but that God could always be trusted to provide for every need and for every good work.

Once, very early in his Christian life, this trust was sorely tested. Brother Andrew was a student at a missionary training school in Scotland. As a Dutchman living abroad, he had to have his visa regularly renewed in order to remain in the country. Now the time had come for his renewal papers to be sent to London, a cost of one shilling—12 pennies.

Brother Andrew did not have a shilling (though he had prayed for it), not even by the morning of the day the papers *had* to be sent. He had also made up his mind that he would not ask others for money in times like these. What would he do? Surely God would not let him be sent away from school for lack of one shilling, would he? At mid-morning, someone came up into the school dorms to report that he had a visitor. Brother Andrew's heart raced. Could this be God's provision?

But as he stepped out of the building, his heart dropped. This was no messenger from God; it was Richard, a man he had met in the slums who sometimes came around to ask for money. As expected, Richard shuffled his feet and asked if Brother Andrew might have any spare cash. As they continued to talk, Brother Andrew noticed a shining shilling lying on the ground. A shilling! He instinctively picked it up and put it in his pocket without Richard seeing.

Then the battle began. This shilling meant that he could send the papers and stay in Scotland to study. But here in front of him was a man in need. Did he really believe in God's Royal Way? He knew what he needed to do. He gave the man the shilling and turned to walk back inside. At that very moment, the postman rounded the corner. In the mail was an envelope carrying more than enough money for his urgent need.[2]

Enough for himself and enough for every good deed—this was the Royal Way. With such confidence, how might you be freed for fearless generosity?

---

[2] Brother Andrew with John and Elizabeth Sherrill, *God's Smuggler* (Old Tappan, NJ: Spire Books, 1967), 70-71.

Questions for Discussion

1. Do you ever fear that you will not have enough resources for the future? Explain. How do your anticipated needs interact with your generosity now? Be practical. The answers may not be easy.

2. For the sake of clarity, work on your understanding of Psalm 112:9, which Paul quotes. What does it mean that "his righteousness endures forever?" Why does Paul quote it?

3. Are you familiar with the "prosperity gospel" movement? In what ways does Paul's teaching differ from it?

4. Have you ever experienced the multiplication of your resources for giving? When you were generous, have you seen God provide more for you to be generous with? Can you relate stories from your own experience or the experience of others?

For the ministry of this service is not only fully supplying the needs of the saints, but is also overflowing through many thanksgivings to God. Because of the proof given by this ministry, they will glorify God for your obedience to your confession of the gospel of Christ and for the liberality of your contribution to them and to all [or, the sincerity of your fellowship toward them and toward all], while they also, by prayer on your behalf, yearn for you because of the surpassing grace of God in you.

2 Corinthians 9:12-14

Chapter Seven

The Sincerity of Your Fellowship

Gifts often do more than meet a need; they communicate. A quick look at the record of diplomatic gifts given to the United States by foreign leaders will remind of you this. Paintings, expensive clothing, jewel-studded daggers, and luxury cars have been sent as expressions of the goodwill of foreign states, though some come with perhaps more subtly ominous symbolism. A few gifts have been quite unusual—such as a baby elephant, a pair of komodo dragons, and the Statue of Liberty—and have had to find homes outside of the national archive.

The point is: gifts mean something.

In this section, we will see explicitly something that Paul has hinted at before: there is a purpose for this collection beyond simply meeting a need. While it is true that the Jerusalem saints are experiencing difficult days and that their need drives Paul's endeavor, he also sees that their need provides a unique opportunity.

The Controversial Gentile Mission

Paul was the spearhead of a remarkable and controversial mission to the Gentile peoples of Asia, Greece, and Italy. He believed he had been personally commissioned by Jesus to take the message of the arrival of Israel's Messiah to non-Jews in these lands. Everywhere he went, he sought to establish believing communities made up of both Jewish and non-Jewish people. As we might imagine, this created a great deal of tension as these people from radically different backgrounds learned to live together as a spiritual family.

What was even more controversial was that Paul maintained that any person, Jew or not, could become a full participant in the Messiah's kingdom and community by decisively believing in him. Even though a Gentile person was coming into a covenant relationship with the God of Israel through the grace of Israel's Messiah, he or she did not have to join in with the Jewish observance of circumcision, food and purity laws, and festivals.

This went off like an explosive in the middle of the fledgling Christian community and occasioned impassioned debate. In the end, all of the Jewish leaders of the Jerusalem church were fully supportive of the Gentile mission (Acts 15). Certain tensions and confusions still remained, however, as witnessed by the fact that many of Paul's letters devote the main part, or at least a major part, to the issue.

Paul was ardent in his quest to achieve unity between the two groups. If God had indeed made "the two into one new man " (Ephesians 2:15), Paul would do all that he could to help them "preserve the unity of the Spirit in the bond of peace" (Ephesians 4:3), both within local congregations and across continents.

So when poverty hit the Jerusalem church, Paul sensed that God was giving him an opportunity to help bring these groups together. We can see how he views the collection in terms of Jew-Gentile relations when we read Romans 15, which he would write just before carrying the collection to Jerusalem. In this passage, he expresses that the Gentiles had a real obligation to the Jewish believers in Jerusalem since their persevering faith had made it possible for the gospel to spread around the Mediterranean world.

> . . . but now, I am going to Jerusalem serving the saints. For Macedonia and Achaia have been pleased to make a contribution for the poor among the saints in Jerusalem. Yes, they were pleased to do so, and they are indebted to them. For if the Gentiles have shared in their spiritual things, they are indebted to minister to them also in material things. (Romans 15:25-27)

Beyond this sense of indebtedness, however, was the opportunity for deepened unity. That is the main thing. Paul believed that a generous gift from the Gentile churches could communicate a message of fellowship and help dissolve some of the barriers between the groups. Follow his logic here in the final section of 2 Corinthians 9.

Thanksgiving for the Gentiles

Paul mentioned in the previous section that God would "increase the harvest of [their] righteousness," which we took to mean that he would "increase the good results that come from their righteous action." What good results are these? He seems to define them, at least in part, as "thanksgiving" in verse 11: "which through us is producing thanksgiving to God." Now in verse 12, he says this even more explicitly. Not only is their liberality meeting the needs of the saints, it is overflowing in its effects by producing *much* thanksgiving to God. Giving of surplus yields gratitude in surplus.

> For the ministry of this service is not only fully supplying the needs of the saints, but is also overflowing through many thanksgivings to God. (2 Corinthians 9:12)

But notice who it is that is giving thanks and what they are thankful for.

> Because of the proof given by this ministry, they will glorify God for your obedience to your confession of the gospel of Christ and for the liberality of your contribution to them and to all . . . (2 Corinthians 9:13)

The Jewish believers in Jerusalem are the ones who will give thanks to God for two things. Pay careful attention to them because they will teach us something important about the potential effects of generosity.

First, Paul anticipates they will thank God for the Gentile believers' obedience to their confession of the gospel of

Christ. This is interesting. Why would he mention this? Are the Jewish believers somehow suspicious that these Gentiles' confession of Jesus is not genuine? Perhaps. In a subtle way, they may have wondered whether this explosion of faith in these former pagans was legitimate, especially when they did not adopt the Jewish customs along with it.

We can see that Paul feels the need to legitimize the Gentiles' faith in his use of the word "proof" ("because of the proof given by this ministry, they will glorify God"). Paul recognizes that if these Gentiles will come through with a sacrificial contribution in their time of need, the Jerusalem Christians will see evidence that their confession of Christ is real. Their generosity will be proof. And the Jewish believers will glorify God for his grace in their lives.

Second, the Jerusalem believers will recognize and be thankful for the sincerity of the Gentile believers' fellowship toward them. The translation we are using reads "they will glorify God . . . for the liberality of your contribution to them and to all," but a different translation seems more fitting in the context. The word for "liberality" sometimes carries the sense of "sincerity," and the word for "contribution" is a common word for "fellowship." The alternative translation, then, might be: "they will glorify God . . . for the sincerity of your fellowship toward them and toward all." Arguments may be convincingly made for either translation, but this is my preference because of Paul's purpose in the paragraph. One good grammatical argument for this translation is that Paul says "to them *and* to all." This only makes sense if we translate the word as "fellowship," and not "contribution," because their contribution was not to "all," but only to the

Jerusalem church. Their fellowship, on the other hand, is extended to the Jerusalem church *and* to all other believers.

The point, therefore, is that the Corinthians' contribution would also furnish proof of their sincere desire for fellowship with the Jewish believers and everyone else. The gift would then become an emblem of mutual acceptance and goodwill between the Jewish and Gentile believers, a great victory and source of glory to God.

Thus the harvest of their generosity will be that the Jerusalem Christians will give thanks to God when they see that the Gentiles' faith and fellowship is genuine. And their recognition of this will not only bring glory to God, but will produce love between them as well, as we see in verse 4.

> . . . while they also, by prayer on your behalf, yearn for you because of the surpassing grace of God in you. (2 Corinthians 9:14)

When the Jerusalem church sees how God's grace is overflowing among the Gentile congregations, they will begin to yearn for them in their prayers. Love and longing will deepen and Paul's mission will truly be accomplished.

Unity for God's Glory: A Harvest of Giving

Giving can do much more than meet needs. It can be an intentional expression of love that overcomes barriers and builds unity.

I have seen this time and again, both as a recipient and a giver. I have watched my love for others and their love for me deepen. That is because giving is a symbolic way of saying, "I care for you." Often, this symbolism is more powerful than words, because it proves that our love goes *beyond* words. More than a nod of the head to sincere fellowship, generosity is a demonstrable proof of our earnest desire for it.

I know of a church that truly understands the potential of strategic generosity. This large congregation has several times given sizable amounts of money to other churches in their city, to meet their needs and to express to them their love. On one particular occasion, the church took up a special collection for a sister church that was just being planted on the same end of town. On the opening Sunday, two of the pastors took the gift to the other church without telling them why they were coming. They arranged a way to be recognized at the end of the service and presented the gift of several thousand dollars. They said, "We love you and want to be the first to invest in what God is doing here." Their only request was that the church who received the gift would "pass it on" somehow when they were more established.

As you might imagine, this was the birth of a special relationship between two congregations who might have felt tension because of their proximity. Their gift was even more meaningful because it was given by an non-denominational church to a Baptist church.

The church that received their gift did indeed "pass it on" in the years that followed. Inspired by the example of their neighbor congregation, they gave 2,000 dollars to a different church in the city every month over a period of two years. The pastor said that they are now friends for life with several of the churches they gave to. He is also aware that at least one of the churches who received money from them has "passed it on" again to five other churches.

This excites me—the idea that we can deploy our surplus in the cause of unity, which Jesus desires deeply for his church. We can use our resources, in fearless generosity, to say to our brothers and sisters, "We love you and we stand beside you in God's new humanity and for God's mission. No matter what the perceived barriers to our fellowship may be, we express to you that we are one Body."

And all of this for the glory of God himself.

Questions for Discussion

Discussion questions for this chapter are found at the end of the following short section. Please discuss this chapter and the final section together.

Thanks be to God for His indescribable gift!

2 Corinthians 9:15

GOD'S INDESCRIBABLE GIFT

A Final Word

This is a book about surplus. On the one hand, it is about *our* surplus—what to do with the extra that God supplies. But more fundamentally, it is about *God's* surplus, the overflow of his grace. As we have seen, he is the real giver.

In these chapters, Paul is compelling us to be fearless givers. We have examined several of his motivations in this book. Some of them make us uncomfortable, testing our assumptions. Others encourage us, inviting us to act on God's promises. But behind each of Paul's motivations is the most transformative motivation of all: God's abundant grace. Of all that we have wrestled with in this book, understanding God's grace has the most potential to launch us into fearless generosity, to push us beyond the constraining caution of cultural Christianity into the new economy of God's supply.

Once more, reflect on this. We saw that it was God himself who enabled the Macedonians to give so sacrificially.

> Now, brethren, we wish to make known to you *the grace of God* which has been given in the churches of Macedonia, that in a great ordeal of affliction their abundance of joy and their deep poverty overflowed in the wealth of their liberality. (2 Corinthians 8:1-2)

It was the sacrificial grace of Jesus Christ toward the Corinthian believers that was to stir them up to a similar act of generosity.

> For you know *the grace of our Lord Jesus Christ*, that though he was rich, yet for your sake he became poor, so that you through his poverty might become rich. (2 Corinthians 8:9)

It was God himself, once again, who promised to provide for their needs without fail, even as they let go of what had formerly been theirs. *And* it was God who would supply for them an abundant and ever increasing surplus as seed for generous planting.

> And God is able to make *all grace* abound to you, so that always having all sufficiency in everything, you may have an abundance for every good deed. (2 Corinthians 9:8)

Finally, it was God himself who would not only meet the needs of others through their giving, but produce a harvest beyond it—of love among believers and thanksgiving to him.

[He will] supply and multiply your seed for sowing and increase the harvest of your righteousness.
(2 Corinthians 9:10)

It is with this harvest of thanksgiving that we conclude. Just as all generosity begins with God and is carried along by God, it ends with God as well, rising again in praises to him. Like the cycle of the rains, it comes down to bless and returns again to the place from which it came.

When we understand that we are caught up in the cycle of God's own liberality, we are freed to undertake acts of radical and strategic generosity ourselves. We can be confident that he has begun the work in our hearts, that he will supply it, and that he will produce a harvest from it. Our generosity does not depend on *our* resources because it is not really our generosity at all. It is God's program that we participate in and *his* resources that are freely given to us and through us.

Give fearlessly. Act on what you have now come to understand—that is, that your generosity is God's work completely. Most are protectors of their resources, and desperate to maintain control. Such people die pitifully, clutching their insignificant treasures. But generosity seen in the new light of God's surplus of grace calls us to let go of control, to count on the abundance of his supply, and to become agents sent to carry out his project of grace.

And so, we end precisely where Paul ends—with what he calls God's "indescribable gift," a phrase that encompasses the whole of God's generous action toward us. We can do nothing but thank him and live our lives now recognizing that he, in his unfathomable grace toward us, is the source and supplier of all generosity.

Thanks be to God for his indescribable gift!
(2 Corinthians 9:15)

Questions for Discussion

1. Do you ever dream of being a more radical and fearless giver? Why?

2. Share stories of times you received gifts that communicated love to you in a special way. Why did such gifts communicate love to you?

3. Brainstorm about ways your church might engage in fearless generosity as a group toward other believers. Do you know of churches that you trust who are in need? How do you think your kindness would impact them?

4. Paul gives us various reasons to be generous in 2 Corinthians 8-9. Here are four from the text: (1) Because God gives us surplus for the express purpose of meeting others' needs. (2) Because God promises to provide for our needs and enough for every good work. (3) Because giving done strategically can result in increased fellowship and unity. (4) Because God's grace initiates, supplies, stimulates, and completes our generosity, for his glory. Of these motivations, which is the most compelling to you? Explain.

2 Corinthians 8-9: Full Text

8:1 Now, brethren, we wish to make known to you the grace of God which has been given in the churches of Macedonia,
2 that in a great ordeal of affliction their abundance of joy and their deep poverty overflowed in the wealth of their liberality.
3 For I testify that according to their ability, and beyond their ability, they gave of their own accord,
4 begging us with much urging for the favor of participation in the support of the saints,
5 and this, not as we had expected, but they first gave themselves to the Lord and to us by the will of God.
6 So we urged Titus that as he had previously made a beginning, so he would also complete in you this gracious work as well.
7 But just as you abound in everything, in faith and utterance and knowledge and in all earnestness and in the love we inspired in you, see that you abound in this gracious work also.
8 I am not speaking this as a command, but as proving through the earnestness of others the sincerity of your love also.
9 For you know the grace of our Lord Jesus Christ, that though He was rich, yet for your sake He became poor, so that you through His poverty might become rich.
10 I give my opinion in this matter, for this is to your advantage, who were the first to begin a year ago not only to do this, but also to desire to do it.
11 But now finish doing it also, so that just as there was the readiness to desire it, so there may be also the completion of it by your ability.

12 For if the readiness is present, it is acceptable according to what a person has, not according to what he does not have.

13 For this is not for the ease of others and for your affliction, but by way of equality—

14 at this present time your abundance being a supply for their need, so that their abundance also may become a supply for your need, that there may be equality;

15 as it is written, "He who gathered much did not have too much and he who gathered little had no lack."

16 But thanks be to God who puts the same earnestness on your behalf in the heart of Titus.

17 For he not only accepted our appeal, but being himself very earnest, he has gone to you of his own accord.

18 We have sent along with him the brother whose fame in the things of the gospel has spread through all the churches;

19 and not only this, but he has also been appointed by the churches to travel with us in this gracious work, which is being administered by us for the glory of the Lord Himself, and to show our readiness,

20 taking precaution so that no one will discredit us in our administration of this generous gift;

21 for we have regard for what is honorable, not only in the sight of the Lord, but also in the sight of men.

22 We have sent with them our brother, whom we have often tested and found diligent in many things, but now even more diligent because of his great confidence in you.

23 As for Titus, he is my partner and fellow worker among you; as for our brethren, they are messengers of the churches, a glory to Christ.

24 Therefore openly before the churches, show them the

proof of your love and of our reason for boasting about you.

9:1 For it is superfluous for me to write to you about this ministry to the saints;

2 for I know your readiness, of which I boast about you to the Macedonians, namely, that Achaia has been prepared since last year, and your zeal has stirred up most of them.

3 But I have sent the brethren, in order that our boasting about you may not be made empty in this case, so that, as I was saying, you may be prepared;

4 otherwise if any Macedonians come with me and find you unprepared, we—not to speak of you—will be put to shame by this confidence.

5 So I thought it necessary to urge the brethren that they would go on ahead to you and arrange beforehand your previously promised bountiful gift, so that the same would be ready as a bountiful gift and not affected by covetousness.

6 Now this I say, he who sows sparingly will also reap sparingly, and he who sows bountifully will also reap bountifully.

7 Each one must do just as he has purposed in his heart, not grudgingly or under compulsion, for God loves a cheerful giver.

8 And God is able to make all grace abound to you, so that always having all sufficiency in everything, you may have an abundance for every good deed;

9 as it is written,

"He scattered abroad, he gave to the poor, his righteousness endures forever."

10 Now He who supplies seed to the sower and bread for food will supply and multiply your seed for sowing and increase the harvest of your righteousness;

11 you will be enriched in everything for all liberality, which through us is producing thanksgiving to God.

12 For the ministry of this service is not only fully supplying the needs of the saints, but is also overflowing through many thanksgivings to God.

13 Because of the proof given by this ministry, they will glorify God for your obedience to your confession of the gospel of Christ and for the liberality of your contribution to them and to all,

14 while they also, by prayer on your behalf, yearn for you because of the surpassing grace of God in you.

15 Thanks be to God for His indescribable gift!